IMAGES
of America

CANE HILL

On the Cover: Pictured are the 1891 Presbyterian church, 1886 Cane Hill College, and 1898 Dr. Blackburn home. All three are listed in the National Register of Historic Places. The development and story of Cane Hill are intertwined with the church and college. (Courtesy the Historic Cane Hill Museum.)

IMAGES
of America
CANE HILL

Bobby R. Braly

Copyright © 2019 by Bobby R. Braly
ISBN 978-1-4671-0382-4

Published by Arcadia Publishing
Charleston, South Carolina

Library of Congress Control Number: 2019932337

For all general information, please contact Arcadia Publishing:
Telephone 843-853-2070
Fax 843-853-0044
E-mail sales@arcadiapublishing.com
For customer service and orders:
Toll-Free 1-888-313-2665

Visit us on the Internet at www.arcadiapublishing.com

For Huxley

CONTENTS

Acknowledgments		6
Introduction		7
1.	The Early Years	9
2.	Places	21
3.	Industry and Agriculture	47
4.	School Days	65
5.	People	109

Acknowledgments

I want to say a heartfelt thank-you to all the individuals and organizations who helped make this book possible. First, the board and staff of Historic Cane Hill were encouraging and supportive throughout the process. The Historic Cane Hill executive board allowed me the time to complete this work, and it is much appreciated. Second, the Shiloh Museum and its staff were invaluable in tracking down several images that appear in this book. Their continued dedication to the history of the Ozarks is to be applauded. Third, I am forever grateful to the Pyeatte, McClellan, Hale, and Irwin families who either allowed me to scan their images or donated images to the Cane Hill Museum. I also appreciate the time spent visiting with so many longtime Cane Hill residents over the last few years learning about their history and the rich details that they contribute to it. This work would not be what it is without that knowledge shared and passed on by people like Dwayne Pyeatte, Betty Colburn, Archie and Irene Reed, Bonnie Haegele, Margaret Loftin, Jeannie Sue McClellan Kisner, and so many more. Thanks to Drs. Kimberly Pyszka and Jerry Hogan for reading an earlier version of this manuscript and providing insightful comments.

When the restoration of Cane Hill started in 2013, I don't think anyone knew what an amazing project it was going to blossom into. The town, descendants of the Cane Hill Community, and the northwest Arkansas area are lucky to see such amazing history preserved. This project and this book would not be possible without the generous support from the Tim and Amy Leach family.

Unless otherwise noted, all images appear courtesy of the Historic Cane Hill Museum.

INTRODUCTION

Cane Hill, Arkansas, was founded in 1827 by Cumberland Presbyterians. These travelers from eastern and central Tennessee and Kentucky were spreading the gospel west by horseback as America itself expanded west. Cane Hill became the first permanent settlement in Washington County, Arkansas, predating Fayetteville. The town went through several name changes during the 19th and early 20th centuries. While the general area is referred to as Cane Hill and the township is still listed as that today, the town itself fluctuated back and forth between Cane Hill, Boonsboro, and Boonsborough several times. The final renaming in 1901 lists it as Canehill. The town quickly developed an identity around four facets of everyday life: religion, education, industry, and agriculture. The Cumberland Presbyterians made a huge impact on the state and region. They established the first public school in the state in 1834 (also claiming the first public library in the state). They also started one of the earliest churches and the first Sunday school in Arkansas. The school evolved into Cane Hill Collegiate Institute in 1850 and Cane Hill College in 1852, one of the state's first institutions for higher learning. Cane Hill Female Seminary was also established in 1852. Cane Hill College enrollment peaked in the late 1850s and early 1860s. The Civil War had a dramatic impact on enrollment, and by 1864, three of four college buildings were destroyed. The college reopened in 1865 following the war, and a replacement wood-frame structure was built in 1868. In 1875, the college admitted women, previously educated south of town at the female seminary, becoming the earliest university in the state to admit and graduate women. In 1885, a fire attributed to arson destroyed the 1868 structure, and the current brick Italianate-style building was built in 1886. The college closed in 1891 and the charter was moved to Clarksville, Arkansas, to start the University of the Ozarks. Following the closure of Cane Hill College, the building reverted back to primary education for grades 1–12 until the 1940s and grades 1–6 until 1956. Following consolidation with the nearby Lincoln School District, the building became a community center, which it continues to serve as today.

The town was also home to an early Methodist population. They were worshiping in the area by 1833, when the first annual conference session of the Methodist Church in Arkansas was held a few miles south of Cane Hill under the direction of Bishop Joshua Soule. In 1859, the Methodist congregation built a substantial brick church in downtown Cane Hill. This population dwindled, and the Methodist church closed in 1904.

In addition to the rich history of education and religion in Cane Hill, the town also has a colorful past that includes amazing architecture (16 properties in the National Register of Historic Places), the Trail of Tears, a Civil War battle, and a long and storied series of commerce and associated merchants and townspeople. During the Trail of Tears removal, several large groups of Native Americans passed through Cane Hill along what is today Highway 45. The B.B. Cannon Treaty Party arrived in Cane Hill on December 26, 1837. The men purchased a coffin from James Coulter and the next day buried Alsey Timberlake, a young Cherokee girl 12 or 13 years old. The Benge detachment of 1,200 Cherokees originated at Fort Payne, Alabama, in September 1838 and passed though Cane Hill in January 1839. At least two of the northern-route detachments under the command of Moses Daniel and Elijah Hicks also passed through Cane Hill in January–March 1839. These two groups numbered 1,035 and 858 individuals respectively when they departed northern Georgia. These routes ended just west of Evansville, Arkansas, near Stilwell, Oklahoma, at the disembarking location known as Mrs. Webber's house.

In the fall of 1862, Cane Hill became home to several Civil War–related encounters, culminating with the Battle of Cane Hill on November 28. In early November, the Confederate Army of the Trans-Mississippi was concentrated around Fort Smith and Van Buren. The summer of 1862 had been harsh and dry. Fall harvests were down, and low water on the Arkansas River made navigation of supplies difficult. Troops were running low on supplies, primarily food rations. Maj. Gen. Thomas Hindman heard of the rich agricultural area of Cane Hill and dispatched Brig.

Gen. John Marmaduke, the cavalry division, and his commissary trains north on November 9. Cane Hill was occupied for five days, and commissary wagons were loaded with meat, flour, hay, and other agricultural goods (likely apples). On the Union side to the north, Brig. Gen. John Schofield stationed Brig. Gen. James Blunt in northwest Arkansas along Flint Creek near present-day Siloam Springs. In late November, Marmaduke made a second trip to Cane Hill with commissary wagons. Union troops under General Blunt mobilized to attack the Confederates on November 27, stopping for the night at Rhea's Mill. On the morning of November 28, General Blunt and about 6,000 Union troops surprised Marmaduke and his approximately 1,800 troops by approaching on Old Fayetteville Road (modern-day Highway 45) rather than the anticipated approach from Old Cincinnati Road (present-day Lincoln–Cane Hill Road). Confederate defensive lines had been placed to the northwest, near the Cane Hill Cemetery. Confederate colonel Joseph "Jo" Shelby and 1,200 men were assigned to guard Cincinnati Road. While Confederate forces were outflanked, a tactical mistake also occurred on the Union side. An infantry unit had been placed ahead of a cavalry unit during the march down the narrow road approaching Cane Hill. This stalled the initial Union attack and allowed the Confederates time to adjust. The initial exchange of artillery fire began near the Cane Hill Cemetery. Outmanned and outgunned, Confederate forces retreated south towards the Cane Hill College grounds and Kidd's Mill. A second defensive position was staged east of Clyde (known as Newburg at the time). Third and fourth defensive positions were also stationed south at Reed's Mountain and along Cove Creek. Confederate forces were driven from the Cane Hill area but not before utilizing a delayed retreat tactic to slow the Union pace and allow commissary wagons to head back to Fort Smith. Overall, Cane Hill was a running battle and considered a Union tactical victory. Brig. Gen. James Blunt then utilized Cane Hill as his headquarters until the Battle of Prairie Grove. Blunt took residence in the redbrick Methodist Manse. The town of Cane Hill was heavily damaged during the battle. Confederate forces, before retreating, destroyed Kidd's Mill. Union forces were also quite proud of their devastation, including the destruction of three of the four large college buildings. A Union soldier noted the damage done by artillery units at the college: "one exploded in the room in which was kept Mathematical, Astronomical, Philosophical, Geographical, etc. etc. instruments" and "that one shell destroyed thousands of dollars' worth of instruments." Union troops then looted the town. Blunt issued orders against these activities and confiscated items from several units, including clothing, blankets, college textbooks, a flute, and a large brass telescope.

Cane Hill remained a bustling community from the 1860s to 1880s, with milling as the primary industry. A local stoneware producer, J.D. Wilbur, manufactured on a regional scale. The economy was driven by agriculture, with apples being one of the most important cash crops. Prior to the Civil War, Cane Hill included a large slave population, which slowly migrated out post–Civil War to nearby Lincoln and south Fayetteville. The postbellum free black community was located just south of town in Happy Holler. The last local descendant, Addie Bryant, passed away in 2004.

During the 1890s, the town began to decline. Plans to construct railroads in northwest Arkansas were met with strong resistance from Cane Hill residents. Gambling, drinking, and prostitution associated with the railroad were considered threats to the Cumberland Presbyterians. By the turn of the century, the railroad was built in Lincoln just to the north. Cane Hill residents were no longer able to compete shipping apples by horse and cart with the train cars. The apple industry then shifted from Cane Hill to Lincoln. The final blows to Cane Hill came in the form of the Great Depression wiping out most of the businesses left in town, followed by a large number of residents who went off to fight in World War II.

In the early 2000s, residents formed an official 501(c)(3) nonprofit, Cane Hill College Association, to care for the deteriorating Cane Hill College building. However, by the late 2000s, most of the community, which contained 15 additional National Register properties, was in serious disrepair. In 2013, the 501(c)(3) was renamed Historic Cane Hill, and a massive preservation project was begun. Major restoration of the town over the last six years has taken the project from a regional site of importance to a state and national audience.

One

THE EARLY YEARS

The early landscape was dotted with small farmsteads. Pioneer settlers brought building techniques and knowledge of architecture styles like Federal and Greek Revival, quickly adapting them to locally available resources with vernacular interpretation. The first settlement included the Old Meeting House, a log structure located near the cemetery that served as the first church and school. This early photograph from around 1884 shows an early Cane Hill College building constructed in 1868.

This Greek Revival structure is the third building constructed on the Cane Hill College campus in 1858. Construction cost was $6,000. It was burned in 1862 during the Civil War. Pictured are Cane Hill College students. The educational program at this time was male only. The coed campus did not begin until 1875.

This photograph from the early 1890s is one of the first depicting Cane Hill College women. Prior to coeducation in 1875, women were educated south of town at the Cane Hill Female Seminary. This photograph was taken just south of the college grounds on the limestone bluffs that run towards the large College Spring, which supplied the town with water.

With the early founding date of Cane Hill, few pictures exist. Thankfully, part of the curriculum at Cane Hill College included drawing and painting. This painting of the 1868 wood-frame college building highlights the town's hilly terrain. The construction of this building served to replace those structures lost in the Civil War. This and the following image both highlight split-rail fencing and the college bell tower.

Another view shows the 1868 college building and bell tower. The bell was brought to Cane Hill in the 1850s after being recovered from the steamship *Grapeshot*, which sank in the Arkansas River. The boat captain was friends with the college faculty and offered it to the newly established school if someone could salvage it. Originally, the bell was housed in one of the three early buildings, but during the Civil War, the building was burned down, and the bell was damaged. (Courtesy Washington County Historical Society.)

This 1874 painting by Molly Mock shows the William McPhetridge house. This house stood on the hill above the college grounds to the northwest. Molly produced this oil on canvas, as well as other sketches, as part of her requirements for the painting and drawing class under the direction of Maj. William "Bill Cush" Quesenbury. The house was one of the residences offered as a boardinghouse to Cane Hill College students.

While some of the first Greek Revival houses still exist today, many early structures have been lost. Thankfully, photographs exist of some of these structures that were lost. This is the old Carnahan place north of Cane Hill. It is a near-copy of the Pyeatte and McClellan houses that still stand today.

Cane Hill musicians are pictured prior to the turn of the century with banjos, fiddles, guitars, and a cello. Music was an integral part of life in Cane Hill. The Cane Hill College curriculum included training in music.

Cane Hill School is depicted about 1910. From left to right are Alice Pyeatte, Nellie Irwin, and Roxa Dismukes on the front steps of the school building.

The Henry Pyeatte home, constructed around 1866, is listed in the National Register of Historic Places. This photograph is from 1908 or 1909. The two men seated on the front porch are Henry Pyeatte (right) and William Moore (left). Two-story and single-story Greek Revival homes became popular during the rebuilding of Cane Hill after the Civil War. They were wood-frame structures with bevel siding. Brick chimneys were usually located at both gable ends.

The McClellan home, listed in the National Register of Historic Places, was built about 1866. Initial construction started prior to 1862, but completion was delayed until after the Civil War. Also designed in the Greek Revival, or I-house, style, it is very similar to the Pyeatte house. Six-over-six double-hung windows dominate the front elevation.

This is the original home of John Rankin Pyeatte and one of the earliest wood-frame structures in Washington County. This house is no longer standing but was located just north of town. The chimneys are still visible west of Highway 45 on the ridge. Adults pictured are, from left to right, Charles Rankin "Charley" Moore, William Smith Moore, Annie Moore, and Lucy Florence Buchanan Moore. They are at Lucy's home in Cane Hill around 1890. (Courtesy Shiloh Museum of Ozark History/Robert F. Richardson Collection, S-2011-63-86.)

This photograph from the late 1890s shows Cane Hill College, the Presbyterian church, and the David Noah Edmiston House (far right). Visible in the foreground is a swinging bridge east of the road. Several of these swinging bridges were constructed throughout town to get residents across Jordan Creek. This bridge led to the Russell place.

A horse and cart are loaded for Sunday church. The individuals in the photograph are unidentified. The Cane Hill Presbyterian Church is visible in the background. It was constructed in 1891 and is listed in the National Register of Historic Places. It was designed in the Gothic Revival style. The Cane Hill Presbyterian Church is considered the mother church for Presbyterianism in northwest Arkansas and traces its root back to the first congregation in town in 1828.

The National Register of Historic Places–listed Cane Hill Presbyterian Church was built in 1891 utilizing native sandstone. This image predates the installation of the stained-glass windows in the 1960s. Also visible is the ornately patterned shingle roof and copper finial located atop the steeple. (Courtesy Shiloh Museum of Ozark History/Martha Moore Collection, S-85-277-50.)

The only remaining structure associated with Cane Hill College is this two-story brick structure. It was built in 1886 and designed in the Italianate style. It was built by Prof. Jacob Carnahan, who had retired in 1883. Construction cost was $5,750. Classes were held again in 1887, but the college closed in 1891.

In this overview of Cane Hill in the 1920s, with a view looking southwest, Cane Hill College is visible in the distance, with several structures also present. The only other identifiable structure still standing is the white house in the right foreground. It was constructed in 1913 and enlarged to two stories in 1918. This served as a residential structure, but it also housed the Cane Hill School lunchroom in the 1930s. (Courtesy Jim Hale/Alfred C. Hale Collection.)

John Sanford Edmiston stands in front of his store on Main Street in Cane Hill around 1910. His two-story native sandstone building was constructed in 1903–1904. It is no longer standing, but some of the foundation remains. Across the street to the left are other similar two-story stone buildings: the A.R. Carroll Drugstore (built in 1900) and the Bank of Cane Hill (built in 1907). All three are vernacular interpretations of a commercial Victorian style. (Courtesy Shiloh Museum of Ozark History/Martha Moore Collection, S-85-277-53.)

With a view looking north on Main Street (Highway 45), this picture was taken about 1910. In addition to the Edmiston General Merchandise store described previously, two additional buildings are visible on the east side of the road in the foreground. Also visible in the middle of the street in the center of downtown is the water fountain.

In this view looking south on Main Street (Highway 45), also taken about 1910, a small blacksmith shop is on the right, along with the large A.R. Carroll Drugstore, two smaller shotgun-style businesses, and the Bank of Cane Hill. Along the left (east) side of the road are a couple of buildings utilized by the Edmiston and Son Canning and Preserving Company and a millinery.

This photograph was taken on September 19, 1907, by H.P. Gould, a horticulturist with the US Department of Agriculture. A heavy apple crop in 1907 drew Gould for a visit. The scene shows numerous wagonloads of apples being unloaded. From left to right, the first building is a warehouse, then J&J Edmiston store (James and John), and a store belonging to the Trout brothers. The next store is the N.E. Tuell Boot and Shoe Shop. The last is a small store operated by Dana Yoe that carried sewing supplies and ladies' hats (millinery).

A c. 1910 view from Booth Campbell's Hill includes Cane Hill College. The photographer's name was Suttle. (Courtesy Shiloh Museum of Ozark History/Martha Moore Collection, S-85-277-55.)

From left to right, E.H. Crowley, John Brewster, and Jim Kirby stand inside E.H. Crowley's store in Cane Hill. (Courtesy Shiloh Museum of Ozark History/Martha Moore Collection, S-85-277-47.)

Two

PLACES

This picture of Cane Hill from the turn of the 20th century stands in contrast to some of the earlier shots of the 19th-century landscape. The town plan has begun to fill in with numerous houses on the landscape, and the downtown area is densely populated. This view, looking northwest, also highlights some of the varied architectural styles of buildings that became locations for many of the historic photographs.

Cane Hill is home to 16 properties listed in the National Register of Historic Places. These buildings, and many others, represent an impressive collection of architectural styles for visitors to enjoy: Greek Revival, Victorian, Italianate, Gothic Revival, Federal, and numerous vernacular interpretations of these. Harry and wife Henry McClellan (lower step on the right), Marion Lee Matthews (lower step center), and Victoria Lipe Kennedy (back left) visit with their family on the front steps of the McClellan house.

The town, from its earliest days, was dominated by a narrow valley cut by Jordan Creek with a high ridge on each side running north–south. The area bounded by these natural features resulted in an elongated townscape. The landscape is dominated by a series of fertile valleys and sandstone and limestone bluffs. Some of the prominent houses, like the Pyeatte house, sit atop these ridges.

Zebulon Brevard Edmiston stands in front of his house in the late 1880s. His wife, Eunice, and daughter Nina are on the front porch. Zeb built the house in 1872 and died in 1891. Later, the house was owned by Dr. E.E. Russell. Dr. Russell operated his optometry clinic from the house.

The Old Dr. Russell Home (Zeb Edmiston house) in Cane Hill is pictured with the Russell family on the front porch. The detailed box columns on the house are visible, along with the front door sidelights and transom. The house is a single-story Greek Revival cottage and still stands on the east side of Highway 45.

This is another example of a Greek Revival cottage in Cane Hill. This is the Bess McClellan house, built by Evan White McClellan. It is no longer standing but was located just south of the college downhill from the lunchroom. The picture is captioned as "The Seven Eaters Club" and includes Henry McClellan, Mrs. Marrs, Bess McClellan, Myrtle McClellan Moore, Mrs. Nicholson, and Mrs. Richardson. (Courtesy Jeannie Sue McClellan Kisner.)

This is another picture of the Bess McClellan home, built by Evan White McClellan. Like that of the Zeb Edmiston house, the front porch is dominated by the Greek Revival architectural details like box columns.

This house sat just south of the Zeb Edmiston house, but it is no longer standing. It is another Greek Revival cottage and was constructed in 1855 by William Blackwell Welch. Dr. Welch served as the surgeon for the 34th Arkansas, Company B, during the Civil War. Upon his return to northwest Arkansas, he sought to professionalize medicine. He was a cofounder of the Washington County Medical Society and the first president of the Arkansas Medical Society. This photograph was taken around 1980.

This photograph of the 1855 William Welch house dates from 1935. Many people know the house as the longtime home of Dr. Conrow Miller. Dr. Miller was the local historian and referred to the house as Reedholme. He passed away in 1987. Many residents sat on Conrow's front porch and got a Cane Hill history lesson. His personal library included over 4,000 books. The house burned about 1998, and the property was purchased by Historic Cane Hill in 2017 to preserve as an archaeological site.

Cane Hill Presbyterian Church is shown in 1936 or 1937. The Gothic Revival–style church was built in 1891, and the flagstone walk in the front was laid as part of the community improvement initiative by the Home Demonstration Club and the church congregation about the time this picture was taken.

This turn-of-the-century postcard offers an interior view of the A.R. Carroll Drugstore. The building was a joint venture when it was constructed in 1900. The lower half was financed by Carroll for his drugstore, and the upper story was financed by the Cane Hill Masons for their Masonic lodge. The postcard is unlabeled, but Carroll is likely standing at the right, behind the counter.

This massive house is the John Sanford Edmiston home, constructed in 1896 in the Queen Anne style with an Eastlake influence. John was the youngest son of Zeb Edmiston and married Alice Lee Lacey. The exterior walls of the house are dominated by imbricated shingles cut into ornate patterns on the second and third floors. The highly styled hexagonal porch draws viewers in with turned columns, arches, sawn balusters, and a spindle frieze.

John Edmiston and his wife, Alice, are seated with their children Clementine, Sam (with wife Edna), and E.W. John Edmiston ran one of the mercantile stores downtown with his brother James (J&J Edmiston General Merchandise), and he ran the family's apple business, the Cane Hill Canning and Evaporating Company. John also served as vice president of the Bank of Cane Hill.

This is one of the few interior shots of any Cane Hill building. The inside of the John Edmiston house was highly decorated, like the highly styled exterior. This is the front, or formal, parlor. A detailed fireplace with tiled hearth dominates the room. The entire house has extensive trim woodwork and wide moldings. Detailed wallpaper and floor coverings are also noticeable.

John Edmiston had a large extended family. He is seated in this picture taken about 1900. Edmiston retired from the bank due to health reasons in 1908 and moved to Washington, DC, where he died in 1916. His wife, Alice, lived another 30 years, and they are both buried in the Edmiston Cemetery in Morrow, Arkansas.

The Bank of Cane Hill was constructed in 1907 and had native sandstone sides with ornamental Victorian pressed tin. The angled front door and numerous finials on the roof gave the bank a unique look. It was located on the corner of Highway 45 and Patterson Road in the center of town. The bank was closed in 1927 when it was purchased by the Bank of Lincoln. Barely in view in the background is the large 24-room Mann Hotel. The hotel is no longer standing.

Another rare interior shot of a building shows the Bank of Cane Hill in the early 1900s. Jim Pyeatte, the cashier at the time, and Alice Edmiston Pyeatte are pictured. The exterior and interior of the bank building were heavily altered in the 1960s; the top half-story with pressed tin was removed, and the front 15 to 20 feet were torn off.

The National Register of Historic Places (NRHP) lists this as the Methodist Manse. This structure first served as a church and then a preacher's residence. It was originally listed in the register as constructed in 1834, but archival research and archaeology revealed a deed and building contract from 1859. The structure was once about three times this size, but it suffered a fire, likely in 1864. It was rebuilt about 1868 to the current size and was restored by Historic Cane Hill in 2017. It also served as the home of Prof. Harrison Welch, president of the Cane Hill Female Seminary. (Author's collection.)

This photograph is captioned "the house that Jane built" and dates to the 1940s. While Cane Hill had several African American residents, few pictures of them exist. Jane earned money in town by doing washing for people. She had a daughter named Patsy who often accompanied her to do laundry at the home of Minnie Cox. The other two children's names are unknown.

This photograph from 1935 shows the home of Wallace Yates. The house was built earlier in the 1920s and is not listed in the National Register of Historic Places. It is located south of town and is in poor condition.

The Campbell home is pictured in 2001. The house was constructed about 1908 and has some Late Victorian influence. It is not NRHP-listed. Most residents know it as the longtime home of Booth Campbell, an accomplished folk musician famous for his work on the banjo. A poet and wallpaper hanger, he was involved early on with the Ozark Folk Festival and won the blue ribbon at the first National Folk Festival. Several of his recordings exist in the University of Arkansas Special Collections.

Downtown Cane Hill is pictured about 1907. Stores include the small shotgun-style Reed General Store in the foreground, with another unidentified shotgun-style business next door. The larger building in the background is the A.R. Carroll Drugstore. This is one of the few early photographs of Cane Hill that shows bicycles. Streets were rough and muddy, making bicycle travel difficult. The view looks to the northwest.

A postcard from the 1930s of downtown Cane Hill depicts the small, shotgun-style building in the foreground that once served as a smithy. The large, two-story structure is the A.R. Carroll Drugstore. One of the two small, shotgun-style buildings seen south of the drugstore in the previous picture has been torn down by this time. The Bank of Cane Hill and an unidentified building to its south are in the background in this southwesterly view.

This Victorian-style cottage was built in 1906 by Dr. John Lacy Bean. Dr. Bean attended Cane Hill College, then the University of Arkansas, and finished his medical degree in St. Louis. He returned to northwest Arkansas to practice medicine and was the first doctor at what is now the Arkansas Country Doctor Museum in Lincoln. This photograph from the early 1900s is labeled "Jim and Zula Huffaker with kids and dogs."

A parade in Cane Hill on August 17, 1968, was photographed by Martha Karnes. The building in the background is the former Bank of Cane Hill after it was altered. It became Jenkins Grocery Store and was run by Charles Ellis Jenkins and Marie Jenkins. (Courtesy Shiloh Museum of Ozark History/Robert F. Richardson Collection, S-2011-63-226.)

Before his store in the old bank building, Jenkins ran a grocery store in the Yates Building to the north. Ellis Jenkins is seated on the left, and the other man and two kids are unidentified. The post office was housed in this building following its departure from the drugstore.

After Jenkins moved his store one building south, Shaker Yates opened a grocery store in the space. Here is the interior of the Yates Grocery with Beecher Lee (left), Myrtle Bullington (center), and Everett Edwards (right). The building was purchased by Historic Cane Hill in 2015 and is the current home of the Cane Hill Museum.

Originally constructed in 1904 as the Edmiston and Son Merchandise Store, this building became the second location for the Clyde Mercantile (ran by Hube Yates) and then served as a short-term home for Shaker Yates Grocery before Yates moved across the street. It was situated on the east side of Highway 45, south of the Zeb Edmiston house, and is no longer standing.

This downtown view of Cane Hill is in March 1968. The Edmiston and Son Merchandise store on the east side of the road is no longer standing. The post office is still in the A.R. Carroll Drugstore building, seen just barely on the right-hand side of the picture (the west side of the road). The drugstore was run by a Mr. Miller at this time.

Downtown Cane Hill is pictured in this northward wintertime view in 1947–1948. This photograph was taken to document the ice storm of January 1948, which local residents still consider the worst winter storm in memory. It made roads impassable. Cane Hill got electricity in 1939, and the town was slowly electrified in the following years, but this storm completely destroyed the town's phone and power lines.

A downtown view looking north shows Cane Hill in August 1947. While Cane Hill got electricity in the 1930s–1940s, the main road through town (Highway 45) was not paved until the 1950s.

Late-1940s downtown Cane Hill is seen in this view from the south. The Bank of Cane Hill, Shaker Yates Grocery Store, and A.R. Carroll Drugstore are all visible on the left (west) side of the road. Clyde Mercantile is visible in the right foreground (the east side of the road). (Courtesy Jeannie Sue McClellan Kisner.)

This late-1940s view of downtown Cane Hill is from the north. Here, the A.R. Carroll Drugstore, Shaker Yates Grocery, and Bank of Cane Hill are all visible on the right (west) side of the road. The Methodist Manse is barely visible through the trees in the far background on the right side of the road. It and the drugstore are listed in the National Register. (Courtesy Jeannie Sue McClellan Kisner.)

The home of Mary Lou and Conrad Russell is pictured around 1935. Conrad would milk cows on the hill and bring milk down to Highway 45 every morning by sleds with a horse. He would stop by the Shaker Yates store at noon for two scoops of ice cream and the mail and then take the sleds back up the hill. This house was torn down, and the board-and-batten siding was used to enclose the front of the former A.R. Carroll Drugstore when it was a barbecue restaurant in the 1980s.

This picture is from 1969 and shows one of the last pre–Civil War slave structures that stood in Cane Hill. This structure from south of town and another north of town near the Pyeatte-Moore house stood until the 1970s–1980s.

This early boardinghouse was utilized by Cane Hill College students. It accommodated 8 to 10 young men each year. An African American man boarded with them and helped with cooking.

This photograph of the log springhouse at Ellen Earle Richardson's was taken about 1935. This was originally the home of Maj. Fountain Earle, who had the house constructed in 1859. Major Earle returned after the Civil War, having served in the 34th Arkansas Infantry, Company B, to be the president of Cane Hill College. Many of the outbuildings in Cane Hill demonstrate unique vernacular architecture.

The well house pictured is at the home of William Welch Yates and Maude Richmond Yates in 1935. William went by "W.W." or "Captain Bill." He and Maude had four sons—Wallace, Stanley, Harry, and James Forrest "Shaker" Yates. Their house was located south of Cane Hill near the Pyeatte-Moore Mill.

A rustic outbuilding in the backyard of Bess McClellan is pictured in 1935. The small-log/stick siding is unique in Cane Hill. Bess lived in a Greek Revival cottage south of the college lunchroom. She died in 1951, and the home sat empty for many years. Charlie Joe McArdell owned it and tore it down in the late 1960s–early 1970s.

Pictured in 1935, this swinging bridge spanned Jordan Creek south of town. The bridge led to the Earle house, home of Ellen Earle Richardson at this time. The man on the bridge is unidentified.

This house was constructed about 1890 by James C. Kirby. It stands on the east side of Highway 45 in downtown Cane Hill. It is in rough shape today and is commonly mistaken for an old barn. Originally, it was a fashionable home built in the Victorian and Italianate styles. Details of the fish scaling in the gable ends and hood molds over the windows are still visible. The house is commonly referred to as the old Colburn home, as Paris Colburn and his family owned the residence for many years.

The home of Stirman and Gladys Karnes is seen before alterations in the early 1930s. This photograph is from a collection dealing with the Cane Hill Club of the Washington County Agriculture Extension Service, College of Agriculture, University of Arkansas, with the US Department of Agriculture cooperating. This collection was from a 1935 Pantry Stores Week sponsored by the club.

This image shows the Karnes home after alterations. This photograph is also from the 1935 Pantry Stores Week. The booklet notes a new kitchen and a bathroom were added, along with indoor plumbing. Three floors were refinished, two rooms were re-papered, a new outbuilding was constructed, one outbuilding was rebuilt, and four flower stands were made. The largest change was the addition of the sleeping porch, which the Karnes family utilized often.

The original James Forrest "Shaker" Yates home was located south of Cane Hill near the Pyeatte-Moore Mill. This house was removed, and a new house was constructed before 1935. This is a distinctive board-and-batten structure with a single central chimney.

The new Forrest "Shaker" Yates home replaced the earlier structure. This photograph was taken about 1935. The two girls on the porch are Sharon and Joann Yates, daughters of Shaker and Helen Garnet Yates.

By the 1980s and 1990s, not much was left of downtown Cane Hill. This shot from September 19, 1999, shows the heavily altered A.R. Carroll Drugstore and the Shaker Yates and Jenkins grocery stores.

The heavy alterations to the A.R. Carroll Drugstore included the addition of a lean-to shed on the north side of the building in the 1980s and the total enclosure of the front porch with a barnwood front by the 1990s. The building became home to the Cane Hill Bar-B-Q restaurant operated by Paul Pahmiyer. This image dates to 2003.

This is one of the earliest close-up pictures of the watering trough, or fountain, at Cane Hill. It shows up from a distance in some of the turn-of-the-century photographs, but this close-up view featuring an unidentified boy and facing north dates to the 1920s. The earliest version of the fountain was oval-shaped and smooth-sided.

By the 1930s, the fountain at Cane Hill had been enlarged to a rectangular shape by adding a rough stone veneer and the words "Cane Hill" on the north and south sides. In this northward view, the drugstore is on the left, with only a few remaining structures on the right.

This view looking southeast shows the Cane Hill fountain with the old Edmiston and Sons General Merchandise store in the background. At this time, the building was home to Clyde Mercantile's second location. Its first store continued to be operated in Clyde, the next town to the south.

The old fountain is in the middle of Highway 45 in the 1940s. The main road through town is still a dirt road at this time, and the spring-fed fountain stands in the middle of the road. This road was paved in the 1950s, and the higher speed traffic forced the townspeople to remove the fountain. The decision was made to save it, and it was relocated to the Cane Hill College grounds, where it still sits today.

Three
INDUSTRY AND AGRICULTURE

The earliest industry in Cane Hill was the cultivation of apples. The earliest settlers from East Tennessee would have brought scion wood and young seedlings with them. This picture from the 1920s shows men sorting, grading, and culling apples in an orchard in Cane Hill. Individuals in the photograph are not identified, but the image does show men and boys across a wide age range, as well as white and African American laborers working alongside one another. (Courtesy Jim Hale/Alfred C. Hale Collection.)

An apple orchard in Cane Hill is in full bloom during the 1920s. Many of the first apple trees were likely planted to support the small household kitchen gardens, but the fruit quickly became commercialized and the town's first cash crop. A nursery was established in 1835 by the Buchanan brothers. The man in this image is unidentified. (Courtesy Jim Hale/Alfred C. Hale Collection.)

The earliest Cane Hill settlers are credited with the development of at least three early varieties of Arkansas apples—Wilson June, Howard Sweet, and Shannon—and many other types were grown in town. The young man is unidentified. (Courtesy Jim Hale/Alfred C. Hale Collection.)

While this picture and the associated previous apple scenes are a bit blurry, they are some of the only images from the heyday of Cane Hill apples. Cane Hill residents fought the arrival of the railroad, and the nearby town of Lincoln got the train station instead. The first train through Lincoln in 1901 was able to ship apples more efficiently than the horse and carts from before. The apple industry then thrived in Lincoln and crashed in Cane Hill. Apples continued to be big business in northwest Arkansas, peaking in 1919 and dwindling significantly over the next few decades. These workers are picking and/or thinning apples in a Cane Hill orchard in the 1920s. This industry was a very labor-intensive undertaking. Growing apples included numerous tasks and associated industries that put large numbers of people to work. Note the horse-drawn wagon and long picking/thinning poles. (Courtesy Jim Hale/Alfred C. Hale Collection.)

Just picking apples wasn't the only thing that was required in the business in 1920s. Wagons and drivers, blacksmiths, stave makers, barrel makers, and a year-round workforce for pruning were required to make orchards run. Apples had to be picked, sorted, washed, peeled, cored, dried, and shipped. The loss of these jobs was devastating to the community's economy. (Courtesy Jim Hale/Alfred C. Hale Collection.)

The second major industry in Cane Hill was milling. By the 1860s, there were at least four mills in operation in the Cane Hill area. While most people think of the Pyeatte-Moore Mill south of town, this is the earlier Pyeatte-Moore Mill when it was located north of town. John Rankin Pyeatte established this mill by the 1830s and, with his son-in-law William S. Moore, expanded it to include steam. The earliest mill in the area is credited to Mark Bean and was located northwest of this location. This photograph was taken around 1927. (Courtesy Shiloh Museum of Ozark History/Robert F. Richardson Collection, S-2011-63-93.)

In this west-facing view is the Pyeatte-Moore Mill just south of downtown Cane Hill that most people are familiar with. The mill was moved to this location in 1902 and operated until the 1920s. Like the earlier version north of town, this mill was able to produce flour and cornmeal, card wool for yarn, and saw logs. It was a large three-story facility with one story built of native sandstone and two stories of wood frame construction. An earlier mill was operated south of this location by Tandy Kidd.

Following the Civil War, William Moore traveled to Cincinnati, Ohio, to purchase new mill equipment. This is an eastward, rear view of the Pyeatte-Moore Mill after several years of deterioration. Water flowed over the top of the wheel in a trough, allowing gravity to assist with the turning of the enormous wheel. The wheel is 3 feet in width and 36 feet in diameter, making it one of the largest overshot wheels in the country.

Flour was one of the most prolific products produced by the mill. Flour from Cane Hill was hauled by horse and wagon across Arkansas and even into Missouri and Oklahoma. After the collapse of the milling industry in Cane Hill in the 1920s, the site became a common place to visit and take pictures. Pictured are Ray and Lois Daugherty. (Courtesy Bob Daugherty.)

A mother and four children are on the west side of the Pyeatte-Moore Mill during the 1920s. While the mill had closed, many of the site's architectural features remained intact for a couple of decades. Lumber was removed and utilized elsewhere, and some of the iron (with the exception of the mill wheel) was removed in the 1940s during World War II for a scrap drive. (Courtesy Jim Hale/Alfred C. Hale Collection.)

Picnicking was a great pastime in Cane Hill, and the millsite was always great to visit and explore. The mother and four children on the west side of the Pyeatte-Moore Mill are not identified. (Courtesy Jim Hale/Alfred C. Hale Collection.)

John Rankin Pyeatte died in 1895, and William Moore then partnered with his son-in-law, Walter Buchanan. When in operation, the large mill could operate off water or steam. Here are four boys playing at the Pyeatte-Moore Mill during the 1920s. (Courtesy Jim Hale/Alfred C. Hale Collection.)

The large mill wheel was heavily damaged by flooding in the early 2000s. It has been removed for preservation and restoration. Letha and Dorris Dean are pictured at the Cane Hill Mill in 1942. (Courtesy Bob Daugherty.)

This picture is captioned "Taken at Cane Hill 1942." The millsite was a common place for couples to visit, picnic, and take pictures. Longtime Washington County historian Walter Lemke described Cane Hill as the most romantic location in the county. Pictured are Ray and Lois Daugherty. (Courtesy Bob Daugherty.)

Part of the infrastructure at the Pyeatte-Moore Mill site included a large retention pond located to the northeast of the actual mill and across the road. The pond and associated mill dam (pictured here during the 1920s) were located on the east side of Highway 45. This structure is still visible in the woods alongside the road. Another early Cane Hill crop, corn, is planted across the road. The landscape at the time was much more open and clear than today. (Courtesy Jim Hale/Alfred C. Hale Collection.)

This close-up photograph of the Pyeatte-Moore millpond shows the interworking of the dam utilized to control water. The large wooden gate could be raised or lowered to control the flow of water through a trough to the overshot wheel. The date of the photograph is unknown, and the three girls are not identified.

The mills in Cane Hill produced large quantities of meal, yet very few pictures of corn growing exist. Thankfully, a few pictures were taken by Cane Hill School agriculture teacher Alfred C. Hale during his time at the school in the 1920s. Here, horses are being used to weed between rows. (Courtesy Jim Hale/Alfred C. Hale Collection.)

Planting and monitoring corn growth was a big part of the agriculture program under Hale at Cane Hill. He kept a detailed journal during his time at the school and documented several additional agriculture projects. Cane Hill's fertile soils and freshwater springs made the town a productive agricultural location for apples, corn, and many other crops. The man in the picture is not identified. (Courtesy Jim Hale/Alfred C. Hale Collection.)

Cattle were another growing agricultural industry in Cane Hill in the 1920s. These three unidentified agriculture students are pictured with a prize bull. (Courtesy Jim Hale/Alfred C. Hale Collection.)

The agriculture students, under the direction of Alfred Hale in the 1920s, won a cattle-judging competition. In the background, barely visible to the left, is the Pyeatte-Moore Mill. (Courtesy Jim Hale/Alfred C. Hale Collection.)

Additional agriculture and industry developed over time. Cane Hill transitioned from apples and grain to cows and chickens. In the 1920s, the fruit industry suffered from disease and drought. Here, agriculture students are constructing a chicken coop on the south lawn of the school building. (Courtesy Jim Hale/Alfred C. Hale Collection.)

During the 1920s, the chicken industry developed and rapidly expanded across northwest Arkansas. In this image, boys from the Cane Hill agriculture class continue framing a chicken coop. (Courtesy Jim Hale/Alfred C. Hale Collection.)

The chicken industry began in northwest Arkansas during the 1890s in Springdale. It would expand rapidly, especially in the 1930s, when other agricultural crops suffered from the Dust Bowl. Here, in the 1920s, agriculture teacher Alfred Hale continues to instruct students on the construction of a chicken coop south of the Cane Hill School building. (Courtesy Jim Hale/Alfred C. Hale Collection.)

This chicken coop was completed in the 1920s south of the Cane Hill school building by the agriculture class. It appears the foundation and part of this structure were used in construction of the lunchroom later during the 1940s. (Courtesy Jim Hale/Alfred C. Hale Collection.)

Jewel Delap Trewhitt was with the Cane Hill Home Demonstration Club of 1936–1937. Jewel noted, "I have 150 birds in my flock and have culled out forty birds. I feed a balance ration, have sold $50 worth of chicken and eggs this year. There are 1075 chickens belonging to club members. 103 birds have been culled this year, Twenty families feed a balanced ration, and one produced broilers for market."

Additional tasks reported by agriculture teacher Alfred Hale in the 1920s included having boys saw trees for lumber. Here, they are working west of the school building. (Courtesy Jim Hale/Alfred C. Hale Collection.)

During the 1935 Better Homes Tour, participants visited the vegetable garden at the home of Gladys and Stirman Karnes. Large kitchen gardens that supported individual households were common. Home canning and a self-sustaining farmstead were necessary.

Another part of the 1935 Home Demonstration Club's program was canning displays. Individuals and businesses alike put their names on jars for viewing purposes. This photograph shows a Ball jar exhibit window in one of the downtown businesses. The image is labeled "Old Mother Hubbard—Modern Mother Hubbard."

Farmers' bounty from a Cane Hill roadside produce stand is pictured. Additional crops grown in town included melons, squash, gourds, apples, and tomatoes. Tomatoes were the last commercial crop in Cane Hill. The Cane Hill Canning Company produced tomatoes up until the 1950s—even though the Great Depression of the 1930s severely curtailed production. (Courtesy Jeannie Sue McClellan Kisner.)

Four

School Days

In 2013, restoration of the Cane Hill College/School building became a focus for Historic Cane Hill and the community. This picture of a primary school class from 1934 shows one of many groups of students that attended school here and created life-long memories. In a town full of great history and amazing architecture, this building has become the symbol of the town. Restoration of the building's 1886 appearance has been dramatic after "modernizations" in 1931 created long-term structural problems from the use of incompatible materials. Restoration of windows, doors, brickwork, chimneys, and a historically appropriate wood shingle roof has brought the building back to life.

Even after Cane Hill College closed in 1891 (it had both a primary and a preparatory department), students like these from around 1895 continued to be educated at Cane Hill School. The Cane Hill School was consolidated with nearby Lincoln in the 1940s and 1950s. The last high school class was held in the 1940s, and the last elementary class was held in 1956. (Courtesy Shiloh Museum of Ozark History/Robert F. Richardson Collection, S-2011-63-167.)

The existing Cane Hill College/School building was constructed in 1886 in the Italianate style of architecture. A brick facade, arched transoms over doorways, and four-over-four light double-hung windows on the first floor and triple-hung windows on the upper floor dominated the exterior. This is a Cane Hill School class from the 1903–1904 school year.

As seen in this postcard image, the building, located just north and west of the downtown commercial area, is massive in scale and dominates the Cane Hill landscape. The large windows helped ventilate the building during warm months. Several windows are open in this view from around the turn of the 20th century.

The Cane Hill School grounds are fairly expansive and cover more than seven acres, mostly to the north of the building. (Courtesy Jim Hale/Alfred C. Hale Collection.)

The Cane Hill College building originally had a front door facing on the east side. A wood shingle roof and large chimneys were part of the original structure.

In 1931, the building was heavily altered during a remodel, and the front door was removed. The building was 45 years old, and many of the original wooden windows had likely deteriorated. While well-intended, these changes created long-term structural problems for the building. Bright-red modern bricks around the replacement windows (likely salvaged from another building) were not toothed in, and hard Portland cement did not mesh well with the original soft lime mortar.

This postcard dating from before the 1931 remodel highlights one of the large trees that still dominates the campus landscape.

This is another early class from Cane Hill School from 1903–1904. Not all of the students are identified, but the teacher seated in front is Nannie Roberts of Pea Ridge. The principal for the year is listed as Dinton Woods, and another teacher, George Woods, is also listed on the back.

This postcard of Cane Hill School dates from 1923–1924. Not all of the pupils are labeled, but the teacher on the right in the second row is agriculture instructor Alfred Hale.

These are senior girls in the Cane Hill School class of 1923–1924. This picture was taken on the southeast corner of the school building. Students would sneak to this back corner and carve their names or initials in the old, soft bricks of the building. Many of these names and initials were preserved during restoration of the building and are in their original locations.

Students at the Cane Hill School in 1923–1924 are pictured with teacher Paul Clifford Davis (back right). This picture was taken on the front steps of the school, which became the predominant place to take class pictures.

In this image of another Cane Hill School class from the 1923–1924 school year, the teacher at right is not identified, and neither are the students. However, Charles Getty McClellan (arms folded) is in the top row at left. (Courtesy Jeannie Sue McClellan Kisner.)

The date of the image on this postcard of Cane Hill schoolchildren is unknown, but it was taken prior to the 1931 remodel of the building. "M. Taylor" likely refers to the teacher or principal for the year.

Cane Hill High School students in a 1920s agriculture class are shown on the front steps of the school building. (Courtesy Jim Hale/Alfred C. Hale Collection.)

The Cane Hill High School students for 1932–1933 are pictured. From left to right are (first row) Marie Yates, Reba Walker, Neva Pennel, Josephine Pyeatte, Ruth Richmond, Merril Karnes, Ramona Copley, Marjie Howell, and Mary Annie Pyeatte; (second row) Mary Louise Pyeatte, Wanda Bittleston, Annie Van Horn, Martha Elizabeth Moore, Janet Marrs, Blanche Sharp, Imogene Hanks, Luella Little, Helen Davis, and teachers Louise Love and Gladys Cullers; (third row) Paul Patterson, Mary Napier, Roddy Davis, Charles Getty McCellan, Howard Low, Alvin Napier, Glen Cox, Virginia Copley, Ivola Ludwick, and teacher D.L. Moore.

This photograph of the Cane Hill School class of 1933–1934 was taken on March 7, 1934. All of the students are identified, but listing their names is beyond the limit of space here. The building had been remodeled by this time, and the picture was made on the steps of the new front door on the north side of the structure.

While the high school students were most commonly photographed, some primary school grades also had their pictures taken. This is the first-grade class at Cane Hill in 1944–1945. (Courtesy Bob Daugherty.)

Cane Hill School's second-grade class photograph for 1944–1945 is shown. The back of the photograph indicates that "John Lulan, Mary Ann, Marry" are pictured. (Courtesy from Bob Daugherty.)

Cane Hill School's third-grade class of 1944–1945 is, from left to right, Ray Braly, Bob Remington, Bonnie Reed Haegele, Rita Belle Tyree, and Gay Braly. Teacher Lois Nolen is not pictured. (Courtesy Bob Daugherty.)

This is the Cane Hill High School senior class of 1944. This is one of only a few photographs with seniors in formal caps and gowns.

Most senior class pictures, like this one from the 1945–1946 class, are far more informal, candid shots taken around the campus. Students are not labeled, but teacher Martha Elizabeth Moore is in the center of the front row, and Wanda Karnes Irwin is just over her right shoulder.

One Cane Hill School tradition is the inscription of graduating seniors' names on the sidewalk in front of the building. This photograph from 1947 includes the Cane Hill High School ninth- and tenth-grade classes.

In this picture from the 1947–1948 Cane Hill School yearbook: the teachers are listed as, from left to right, Martha E. Moore (English), Sue Skinner (fourth–sixth grades), Jennee J. Shoemaker (first–third grades), Mrs. J.O. Skinner (science and math), and David Leonidis "Lon" Moore (political science).

Pictures of younger grades, particularly elementary-age students, are far less common. This image shows the Cane Hill School first-, second-, and third-grade classes in 1949. Note the additional pupil in the back row center, a girl's doll that had to make the shot.

The Cane Hill High School class of 1949 is pictured. Members are, from left to right, (first row) Joann Yates, Mary Lee Grant, and Verna Pitts; (second row) Leroy Willis, Wanda Karnes Irwin, and Tommy Rogers.

One of the traditions in Cane Hill is the all-school reunion, held the fourth weekend in September. Here is the same class of 1949 (with a few extras) at a reunion in 1989. Identified in the picture are "Tommy Rogers, Louise, Mary, John, Dorothy, Joann, Verna, Allyne, Margaret Loftin, and Marth E. Moore."

Snow covers the grounds of Cane Hill School in the 1920s. Snow always makes for beautiful scenes like this in Cane Hill. The view is toward the south through the large walnut trees planted by Major Earle in 1896. (Courtesy Jim Hale/Alfred C. Hale Collection.)

Wintertime activities abounded on the school campus, seen in this view looking northwest. A snow day in the 1920s on the grounds of the Cane Hill School building included sledding down the many hills. (Courtesy Jim Hale/Alfred C. Hale Collection.)

Snow days on the grounds of the Cane Hill School also included building a snowman. The John Edmiston house is visible in the background. Taken in the 1920s, this view faces north. (Courtesy Jim Hale/Alfred C. Hale Collection.)

Here, construction of the snowman has halted for a snowball fight. The Edmiston house is visible in the background of this view as well. (Courtesy Jim Hale/Alfred C. Hale Collection.)

This snow day in the 1920s at Cane Hill School also included an impromptu take on ice-skating. No special shoes or skates were used. Snow was packed to form a solid icy layer, and students took turns sliding down the track. (Courtesy Jim Hale/Alfred C. Hale Collection.)

Other Cane Hill School activities included a class picnic. Here, Mary Francis Patrick (left) and Joann Yates (right) wait to board the bus for a class trip in the late 1940s. Other school activities included class plays, carnivals (often at Halloween), potlucks, roller-skating together in Fayetteville, and a wiener roast (often held at Cold Springs north of town).

A picture taken in February 1947 on the southeast corner of the school building shows, from left to right, Louise Biggs, Allene Karnes, and Joann Yates. By the late 1940s, the building and grounds were suffering from disrepair. Notice the stone wall, a common feature throughout Cane Hill, is missing most of the mortar in the joints.

From left to right, Mary Francis Patrick, Leroy Willis, and Joann Yates are on the school playground south of the school building. The students are waiting around outside to go on the 1947 school picnic.

From left to right, Billy Hossman, Mary Lee Grant, Gordon Elliot, Margaret Holden Loftin, Leroy Willis, and Mary Francis Patrick are waiting to board the bus in another image taken before the 1947 Cane Hill School picnic.

A swing set, slide, and merry-go-round were all on the Cane Hill School playground. Louise Biggs, Connie Delap, Margaret Holden Loftin, Dix Foster, and Billy Hossman wait to leave for the 1947 school picnic.

Wayne Willis is pictured in the Cane Hill yearbook. He was senior class president in 1947–1948. He participated in basketball and the 1948 senior play. Wayne and Richard Kost both joined the military during World War II and returned to Cane Hill High School to complete their educations after the war—quite an honorable undertaking. Wayne served in the armed forces from September 1945 until May 1947 and returned to Cane Hill for his senior year with the rank of sergeant.

Louise Biggs (left) and Mary Lee Grant are on the merry-go-round south of the school building in 1947. The merry-go-round is still at this location on the campus.

Louise Biggs (left) and Mary Francis Patrick are pictured. When asked about this picture, taken in February 1947, Margaret Holden Loftin noted that Louise was "just pretending to be smoking one of the boy's cigarettes."

Seniors in the 1947–1948 class at Cane Hill, like many before them, put on a play for the entire school. The play that year was entitled *Girls Are Like That*. Here are two seniors from that class, Mary Lee Grant (left) and Joann Yates. Grant was the star of the play on March 26, 1948.

The 1947–1948 senior class banquet (put on by the junior class) was held on April 14, and the school picnic was held in February 1948. Commencement occurred on April 23, 1948. In this view facing west, Louise Biggs (left) and Joann Yates are pictured in front of the Cane Hill School building in February 1948.

From left to right, Louise Biggs, Mary Francis Patrick, and Joann Yates are dressed up for the 1947 Cane Hill School picnic. Like at many schools, students participated in Who's Who. Mary Francis was voted "Most Popular," and Joann was voted "Best All Around Girl."

A bus was not utilized every day in Cane Hill. Only on special occasions did the school use one, and it was borrowed from Lincoln. Here, from left to right, Connie Delap, Dix Foster, Tommy Rogers (front), Joann Yates, Louise Biggs, Mary Francis Patrick, Billy Hossman, and Leroy Willis (front) are about to board the bus for the 1947 Cane Hill School picnic.

Cane Hill School agriculture students participated in numerous activities around the campus and contributed to the school's infrastructure. Here, students and staff in the 1920s are framing up the boys' and girls' outhouses on the hill above the school building. Look carefully to see one of the boys under the structure digging the hole for the toilet. While these outhouses no longer exist, they were located on the hill above the building, very near to the current restrooms. (Courtesy Jim Hale/Alfred C. Hale Collection.)

Another extracurricular activity common at Cane Hill School was participation in the agriculture program. Cane Hill has a long and rich agricultural heritage, and the agriculture program at the school was an excellent one. This is one of the Cane Hill School agriculture classes from the 1920s. Seen here in the center of the back row, Alfred C. Hale was the instructor. (Courtesy Jim Hale/Alfred C. Hale Collection.)

The agriculture class also constructed this unidentified concrete feature on the southwest corner of the building in the 1920s. Its use is unknown, but it was encountered during college restoration in 2016. (Courtesy Jim Hale/Alfred C. Hale Collection.)

One big accomplishment of the agriculture class was leveling of the grounds north of the building for improvements to the basketball court. Here, a team of horses is used to smooth the ground for two basketball courts. (Courtesy Jim Hale/Alfred C. Hale Collection.)

Two unidentified boys from agriculture class are removing trees on the Cane Hill School grounds just west of the Cane Hill College building. Also in view in this picture is repair work being undertaken on the bell tower. In this and many other depictions of the structure, boards are missing and/or paint is peeling. Maintaining the tower is a struggle still today, which is thought be in part due to its unique shape. (Courtesy Jim Hale/Alfred C. Hale Collection.)

Basketball became a huge part of Cane Hill School. This is one of the earliest known basketball pictures and shows the boys' team from the 1920s. (Courtesy Jim Hale/Alfred C. Hale Collection.)

The Cane Hill Senior High boys' basketball team is on the court in 1945. Players include Francis Taylor, Smokey Mourning, Wesley Young, Warren Kost, Eugene Holden, Buck Jones, Wayne Crawford, and John Skinner.

The Cane Hill Senior High boys' basketball team poses on the steps of the school building in 1945. A full list of pupils is on the back of the photograph. Identified from left to right are Wesley Young, Smokey Mourning, Francis Taylor, Warren Kost, John Skinner, Eugene Holden, Buck Jones, and Leon or Wayne Crawford.

The Cane Hill College campus grounds by the 1920s included a volleyball/tennis net and two basketball courts with a set of gymnastic rings between them. (Courtesy Jim Hale/Alfred C. Hale Collection.)

This is the Cane Hill High School boys' basketball team for 1946–1947. In 1942, the first class of boys played "touch ball," or touch football. Although no pictures are known of the activity, it is listed in the Cane Hill School yearbooks.

Cane Hill Junior High boys' basketball players in 1945–1946 are, from left to right, (first row) Leroy Willis, Tommy Rogers, and Johnnie Carte; the second row includes Charlie Hobbs, Johnny Jones, and Connie Delap.

The Cane Hill boys' basketball in 1945–1946 had Martha Elizabeth Moore as coach. Another sport added to the physical education program at Cane Hill School in the 1940s was Ping-Pong.

Cane Hill's boys' basketball team for 1945–1946 includes, from left to right, John Skinner, Buck Jones, Leon Crawford, Eugene Holden, Leon Gardisser, Richard McClain, Wesley Young, Warren Kost, and Smokey Mourning. Coach Martha Elizabeth Moore is not pictured.

The Cane Hill Senior High boys' basketball team for 1945–1946 received three trophies—second place at the county tournament, Sportsmanship Award at the county tournament, and second place at the West Fork tournament. Pictured from left to right are John Skinner, Richard McClain, Leon Gardisser, Leon Crawford, Buck Jones, Eugene Holden, Warren Kost, Smokey Mourning, and Wesley Young.

The Cane Hill junior boys' basketball players and coach in 1949 include D.L. Moore (coach), David Redway (7), Pete Gibbs (8), Theron Woods (9), Bobby Vanderpool (10), Danny Irwin (11), and Bob Remington (2).

A photograph of Cane Hill senior boys' basketball players and their coach in 1949 includes D.L. Moore (coach), Rex Curry (5), Johnny Jones (9), Leroy Willis (14), Gordon Elliot (12), Connie Delap (2), and Robert Patrick (4).

Girls' basketball was just as popular in Cane Hill at boys' basketball, if not more so. This is the Cane Hill High School girls' team photograph from 1943–1944. Pictured from left to right are Allene "Sis" Karnes, Dorothy Yates, Carol Lee Matthews, Wanda Karnes, coach Mildred Welchel, Reba Delap, Loretta Remington, Patti Trewhitt, Mary Patrick, and ? Collins.

In this photograph of the Cane Hill girls' basketball for 1945–1946 are, from left to right, (first row) Frances Keene, Kathlene Reed, Allene Rogers, Louise Biggs, and coach Marie Yates Benton; the second row includes Neva Jean Sharp, Rhea Norwood, and Wilma Brassier.

The Cane Hill girls' basketball team from 1945–1946 includes, from left to right, (first row) Dorothy Yates, Patie Teewhitt, Wanda Karnes, and Verna Pitt; (second row) Wanda Brasier, Margaret Holden, Joann Yates, and Joy Copley; (third row) Neva Jean Sharp, Reba Dee Spinks, and coach Marie Yates Benton.

The Cane Hill High School girls' basketball from 1945–1946 poses in front of the school building. The girls' team received one trophy that year. These trophies accumulated over the years and are housed in the Cane Hill Museum.

While Cane Hill did not have an actual physical mascot, teams were known as the Blue Racers. Team colors were blue and white. The Cane Hill High School girls' basketball team from 1946–1947 is pictured.

This image shows the Cane Hill High School girls' basketball team in April 1947 on its home court. The walnut trees in the background, planted by Major Earle in 1896, would have been 50 years old at this point. They still stand tall on the school grounds.

The Cane Hill High School girls' basketball team from April 1947 is on the Cane Hill basketball court. The flat spot where this court stood is still visible on the grounds today just north of the building. Playing outside on dirt courts was common at this time.

The Cane Hill High School Blue Racers take the court for practice in April 1947. The *Blue Arrow* was the name of the school's annual yearbook.

The guard position was one of the most important on the basketball team, as a guard was often the coach on the floor and leader of the team. Cane Hill had a bumper crop of guards in the 1947 season. In this view facing west, all of the guards stand in front of the school building.

From left to right, Joann Yates, Margaret Holden, and Louise Biggs are in this photograph taken in April 1947 with one of the best views of the basketball goal and backboard. Also note the bell tower in the background and the damaged paint and missing boards. Maintenance of this structure continues to be problematic, likely due to the tapered shape.

Wanda Irwin graduated from Cane Hill High School in 1946. She returned to the school to teach and coach basketball. She is at far right with her team from the 1948–1949 school year.

The Cane Hill High School boys' basketball team from the 1948–1949 school year is pictured in the background. The coaches are Martha E. Moore (left) and Wanda Irwin.

The photographer is lining up the 1948–1949 Cane Hill High School Blue Racers. Coach Wanda Irwin is at right.

The basketball court was also a hangout area for students like Gordon Elliot when a game or practice was not going on. This view from 1949 looks northwest.

This picture from 1949 is the only known image of the Cane Hill School grounds showing the baseball field in the far northwest corner of the campus (left side of the picture). One story is that a student once hit a baseball all the way over the building. Both boys and girls also fielded softball teams for Cane Hill School. In the picture, Margaret Holden and Joann Yates are on the basketball court, facing away from the camera.

Among the richest and longest-lasting treasures of Cane Hill are its people. They are one of the things that make Cane Hill great. So many individuals have been proud descendants of the town and its rich history. Here, Arling McClellan and Martha Elizabeth Moore participate in a Tom Thumb wedding as part of the 1927 centennial celebration of the founding of Cane Hill.

Five

PEOPLE

People are pictured in the street at the north end of Cane Hill around 1910. The Blackburn house and Presbyterian church are barely visible in the background. There are deep ruts in Main Street. (Courtesy Shiloh Museum of Ozark History/Martha Moore Collection, S-85-277-56.)

This photograph from the 1935 Cane Hill Club of the Washington County Agriculture Extension Service, College of Agriculture, University of Arkansas, is captioned "Improvements at the home of S.E. Marrs include one bird bath built." This is in the backyard of the National Register of Historic Places–listed 1886 Dr. Blackburn house. The bird bath is still standing. The two children are unidentified.

In 1935, during the Home Demonstration Club, Bess McClellan's backyard took first prize in the yard and garden contest. Her home, a Greek Revival cottage located south of the school lunchroom, is no longer standing.

Martha Elizabeth Moore was one of the longtime teachers at Cane Hill School. She was a lifelong resident of Cane Hill. Many students had fond memories of her, like the distinctive red hood she wore, seen in this photograph taken in February 1947.

This photograph shows Sue Skinner in front of the Kirby/Colburn house in January 1947. Sue was the daughter of the Reverend J.O. Skinner, longtime preacher of the Cane Hill Presbyterian Church.

Many residents of Cane Hill were proud of their history and would tell stories relayed on from generations before. Individuals who were unofficial town historians included Conrow Miller and Conrad Russell, pictured here in 1973.

Visiting outdoors was common practice. Front porches and backyards were centers for community activities in Cane Hill. Conrow Miller was known for hosting formal parties in his backyard. Here, Bess McClellan shows off the outdoor living room at her house just south of the college. The photograph was taken in 1935.

Gatherings of families and friends became a recurrent theme in Cane Hill. One of the earliest and largest was the 1927 Centennial Celebration of the founding of Cane Hill. Here is a scene from the 1927 pageant that took place in front of the William Welch home, where Conrow Miller lived. (Courtesy Jeannie Sue McClellan Kisner.)

Louise McClellan, Martha E. Moore, Bess McClellan, Charles G. McClellan, and Myrtle Belle Carrol are pictured with grandmother Lizzy Cowley McClellan. (Courtesy Jeannie Sue McClellan Kisner.)

The 1935 Home Demonstration Club Better Homes Tour included a "place of interest" stop at the sleeping porch of Mrs. Charles Delap north of town. Prior to electricity and cooling systems, houses did not cool down as quickly as the porch in warm summer months. As such, these enclosed porches were common in Cane Hill from the 1920s onward. Porches became the hub for community news and gossip.

Church functions drew large crowds of people together, like in this scene from the 1940s or 1950s. The 1891 Cane Hill Presbyterian Church, pictured here, originally had clear glass windows. The stained glass was added in the 1960s. A rear annex for a fellowship hall was added in the 1960s as well.

The back sides of buildings were rarely photographed in Cane Hill. Here, Smokey Mourning and John Skinner (right) are behind the Presbyterian church in January 1947. Many people think the apse, or location of the altar and clergy, is beautifully executed and worth walking around to see.

Charles Getty "Get" McClellan, age 10, and his dog Gussie are pictured about 1925. Dogs were, of course, common in Cane Hill, but they rarely made it into pictures. In Cane Hill, dogs were heavily utilized in hunting and trapping. Men commonly sought squirrels, raccoons, foxes, and bobcats with dogs. Some of the women suggested it was really an opportunity to get out of the house and drink.

A turn-of-the-20th-century photograph features a dog in Cane Hill. The three men walking south along College Road are unidentified. The National Register of Historic Places–listed Cane Hill College building is visible in the background.

Two unidentified men with their dog are sitting in front of the John Edmiston house. Built in 1896, the home is now listed in the National Register of Historic Places.

Agriculture teacher Alfred Hale arranged for neighboring school principals and politicians to visit the Cane Hill campus and see the many improvements his students had accomplished. These unidentified men are visiting the Cane Hill School agriculture class in the 1920s. (Courtesy Jim Hale/Alfred C. Hale Collection.)

Other common social activities were family reunions and community picnics. This photograph taken about 1907 shows the Moore family picnic held at the J. Moore home. Included on the photograph caption is "Uncle Jerry's Boys, M. Hodge, David, Holt, Aunt Mary Moore—Aunt Ann's sister."

This McClellan family reunion picture from the 1920s was made on the Cane Hill College grounds. The college building in the background was constructed in 1886. The original Italianate windows are visible in this picture, but they were even then in poor condition. The window on the right has a board substituting for the lower left pane of glass. These windows were all removed in a massive remodel in 1931.

A large picnic at the Joseph H. Moore house includes members from the Buchanan, Pyeatte, Ross, Moore, Murray, Brewster, Spears, McClain, Gould, Bullen, Crain, Inks, Babb, Robinson, Wilson, Black, Allen, Crawford, and Patterson families. (Courtesy Shiloh Museum of Ozark History/Martha Moore Collection, S-85-277-46.)

A picnic in 1935 at the Presbyterian manse is pictured. Not to be confused with the Methodist Manse south of town, the Presbyterian preacher's residence was the 1898 Dr. Blackburn house, now listed in the National Register and still standing. The house at the time would have been occupied by preacher Sam Marrs and his family until he traded churches with J.O. Skinner in 1938.

This image shows part of the 1935 Home Demonstration Club Better Home Tour and Program. This was an all-day meeting and program at Cane Hill Presbyterian Church with a picnic on the church lawn served by the Cane Hill Club at noon.

This is another shot of the 1935 Home Demonstration Club Better Home Tour and Program picnic on the Presbyterian church lawn. The church served as the central spiritual and social hub of the community. A variety of events was often held at the church and next door at the preacher's residence.

This is a rare photograph of one of the African American members of Cane Hill. Clara Smith poses on the front steps of the McClellan house. Clara and her husband, Homer, lived just east of the McClellan house in a small white home near Addie and Dude Bryant's.

Another African American resident, Don Trout, lived with the Brewster family. When the Brewster, Pyeatte, and Buchanan boys attended the University of Arkansas, Don went along to keep house and cook at the boardinghouse where they lived.

An unidentified couple in the 1920s poses by Happy Holler Falls, located south of town and east of Highway 45 and the Pyeatte-Moore Mill. The area above these falls on Happy Holler Road was where the original road ran prior to paving. The large sandstone rocks above the falls are flat and smooth, making for easy crossing when water is not high.

A couple stands under the arbor at a brush arbor revival in Cane Hill on August 17, 1968. Martha Karnes was the photographer. (Courtesy Shiloh Museum of Ozark History/Robert F. Richardson Collection, S-2011-63-222.)

One of the largest and most enduring gatherings of people in Cane Hill is the annual festival. Originally titled Old Pioneer Days, it started in the 1960s and was held during the spring. Due to the constant rain, the event was moved to the fall and became the Cane Hill Harvest Festival. The event is still held every year on the school grounds during the third week in September. This shot is an overview of the Cane Hill Harvest Festival in 1998.

Cane Hill Harvest Festival goers visit underneath a shade tree in 1998. Events at the festival include sorghum molasses, apple, butter, lye soap, and hominy production. Music, dancing, and fair food are all included activities during the festival.

One of the greatest things that the Cane Hill Harvest Festival does is bring people together. Some of the last students that attended Cane Hill School return for the festival and the all-school reunion the following weekend. Here are, from left to right, Joann Yates, Mary Francis Patrick, Jessie Woods, Bessie Woods, Margaret Holden Loftin, Verna Pitts, Wanda Brashier, and Wanda Karnes Irwin on the basketball court they played on in the 1940s during the 2002 reunion.

Pictured here are some students who attended Cane Hill School 50 years before. From left to right, Louise Biggs, Leroy Willis, Mary Francis Patrick, Margaret Holden Loftin, Mary Lee Grant, Joann Yates, Verna Pitts, Tommy Rodgers, Marvin Matthews, and Martha E. Moore are at the all-school reunion in 1990.

Another great tradition of the Cane Hill Festival is the quilt show. Quilting has a long tradition in Cane Hill, and pictured here in September 1998 are Mary Rice (left) and Martha Elizabeth Moore. Rice lived in the white house north of the college grounds during the 1970s and had a passion for quilts. These two ladies were stalwarts of the preservation of Cane Hill. It is because of them, and many others going back several generations, that the town and its history have survived.

Visit us at
arcadiapublishing.com

www.ingramcontent.com/pod-product-compliance
Lightning Source LLC
Chambersburg PA
CBHW060937170426
43194CB00027B/2980